Fun Crafts
FOR KiDS

Written and compiled by Jennie Mackenzie

Fun CRAFTS FOR KIDS

There is an ever-growing understanding of the importance of creative arts and crafts for young children. Parents and educators appreciate the need to provide opportunities for self expression, the use of imagination and achievements that reflect the growth of important physical skills. Children of every age benefit from the activities which develop awareness through observation, touch, smell and hearing.

These pages are for everyone who spends time with, and cares for, young children. The activities presented are intended only as a guide. Be sensitive to your children's own ideas and adapt our methods to them and to your available resources. And **please** don't let children copy directly from the book, but encourage them to experiment, and 'do their own thing'!

The activities described here can be done by most four year olds. You will often need to simplify tasks for a two year old, though a three year old may be able to manage them with little or no help. Encourage older children to use the activities as a starting point for extending their own level of skill. With most activities we have included a section called **Other things to try** which often include ideas for older children, as well as adding variety to simple activities for the younger child.

The crafts are grouped according to type rather than skill level but where possible, the most simple one comes first in each group. Each activity begins with HAVE READY which will list your ingredients, followed by GET SET which lists the steps for preparation and finally comes the fun part, GO!

Steps marked * need to be performed by an adult or at least supervised, depending on your child and the particular situation.

One secret for successful creative play is 'be prepared'. Find a place where mess doesn't matter so much and where unfinished work can be left to be completed later. Keep a box of old clothes, plastic sheeting and any other bits and pieces you think might come in handy, like cardboard rolls, bits of foil and fabric, lengths of coloured yarn and so on. Your rubbish can be a young child's art material and treasure.

Perhaps the most important ingredient in the process is FUN! This book is all about having fun in a creative way and sharing these good experiences with your child.

Jennie Mackenzie

CONTENTS

EDITORIAL
Managing Editor: Judy Poulos
Editorial Co-ordinator: Margaret Kelly

DESIGN AND PRODUCTION
Amanda Westwood; Nadia Sbisa;
Margie Mulray; Chris Hatcher

COVER
Design: Frank Pithers

PHOTOGRAPHY
Andrew Elton

PUBLISHER
Philippa Sandall

Family Circle is a registered trademark of
IPC Magazines Ltd.
Published by J. B. Fairfax Press Pty Ltd by
arrangement with IPC Magazines Ltd

Fun Crafts for Kids
ISBN 1 86343 015 6
Formatted by J.B. Fairfax Press Pty Ltd
Output by Adtype, Sydney
Printed by Toppan Printing Co, Hong Kong
Distributed by J.B. Fairfax Ltd
9 Trinity Centre, Park Farm Estate,
Wellingborough, Northants.
Ph: (0933) 402330 Fax: (0933) 402234

PAINTING

Painting opens up a child's world of colour and imagination. Children revel in the experience of brushing, spattering, dripping, squeezing and squelching paint on paper. The resulting picture is much less important than the creative process and the enjoyment of the experience.

The first stage of painting lies in the joy of experimenting with colour. You need only provide the equipment, opportunity and encouragement, then stand back and let it all happen!

Painting is bound to make quite a mess — so be prepared. Find a spot where paint splashes don't matter or 'carpet' the area with layers of newspaper. A painting apron is a good idea but one of dad's old shirts will do just as well. Have a bucket or bowl of soapy water and a sponge at hand for cleaning up drips and splashes.

Very young children prefer to paint sitting down on the floor or standing at a low table. An older child often feels more comfortable with an easel. Of course you don't have to rush out and buy an easel — simply find a place where you can tape, peg or pin (with some child-proof drawing pins) some paper at the appropriate height. Find a suitable spot for the painting to hang until dry.

What you need

Brushes Brushes should have long fairly thick handles which are easy for a child to control. Start with some quite thick brushes (200-250 mm) and add finer brushes later on. If possible have one brush for each colour or provide clean water and a cloth for rinsing brushes between colours. Teach your child how to clean the brushes after painting and to store them, with bristles standing up, in a jar or bottle.

Paints Paint for young children must be absolutely safe. Whether you choose powdered or ready-mixed paints, make sure that they are clearly marked *non-toxic*. Start with the basic colours of red, yellow and blue with black and white. Mixing these will provide a variety of colours and, with the addition of white or black, you can also vary the tone. Don't forget to make grey as well.

Paper Children prefer to work on fairly large sheets of paper, about 60 cm x 75 cm. Remember that providing backgrounds of different colours and sizes can offer a whole new avenue for your child to explore. Collect suitable paper for use later. Printers and paper mills often let you have bits and pieces. Architects and engineers may have old plans, blank on one side, and offices are often delighted to get rid of unwanted computer printouts.

Containers Any old jar, cup or plastic container is quite suitable, providing it is clean and will not topple over when a brush is left standing in it. Remember not to overfill the container. 2-3 cm of paint is quite sufficient.

Colourings Edible vegetable dyes are available from toy shops and art suppliers in powder form. Colours are strong but there is no effective black or white. To use, first dissolve a small quantity of the powder in a tablespoon of water before adding it to cornflour paste, starch or wallpaper paste to make a thick paint suitable for brush painting.

Food colourings are available from supermarkets and food stores in liquid form. The colours are not as strong as the vegetable dyes. To use, mix them in the same way   as vegetable dyes.

Tempera is a non-toxic powdered paint available at artists' suppliers. It comes in a wide variety of strong colours, including black and white. Tempera is more opaque than the vegetable dyes and because it dries quite quickly colours can be overlaid more easily. To use, mix powder with a little water to form a paste then add the rest of the water. Generally a ratio of two-thirds powder to one-third water gives the best result. You can add starch or paste to increase the volume but the colour will be more transparent and the paint may flake off when dry.

Covers and protectors These can be made from a variety of materials, from newspapers, plastic sheets (including old shower curtains or raincoats) to unwanted bed linen. The cheapest and most accessible covering for tables and floor is of course plain old newspaper. Remember that a disposable cover is preferable to one that requires washing. A painting apron or some similar covering saves a lot of bother on washday.

■ Painting on paper

● HAVE READY
paint
brushes
large sheet of paper
● GET SET
Protect floor area.
Position containers of paint and brushes in a safe position close to paper.
Secure paper in position (if necessary).
● GO
When finished hang painting somewhere safe to dry.

■ Easel painting

● HAVE READY
paint
brushes
easel, board or suitable wall surface
pegs; bulldog clips; drawing pins or tape
● GET SET
Protect floor area.
Position paint and brushes in convenient place, close to easel.
Secure paper to easel with pegs, clips or tape.
● GO
When finished hang painting somewhere safe to dry.

■ *Object painting*

● HAVE READY
paint
brushes
large paper
easel or board
pegs, clips or tape
objects such as sticks,
feathers; rope; sponge;
cotton wool balls; nails;
shaving brushes; dishmops
and so on
● GET SET
Set up as for *Easel
painting.*
● GO

Other things to try

■ **Provide several tones of only
one colour plus black and white.**
■ **Let colours set a theme such as
sunny, cold, happy or sad.**
■ **Vary the shape and size of the
paper. Try different colours and
textures of paper including
wallpaper, wrapping paper, waxed
and absorbent paper, boxes and
paper bags.**
■ **Make the paint watery or add
sand, detergent, salt or sugar for
different effects.**
■ **For older children try paper
with patterns or holes in it.**

■ *Water painting*

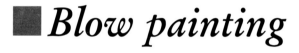

● HAVE READY
bucket or bowl
broad brush
water
● GET SET
Fill bucket with water.
Find a suitable surface for
painting such as paths,
walls, fences and so on.
And there is no cleaning
up or mess! Young
painters find this very
satisfying.
● GO

Other things to try
■ **Use paint rollers.**
■ **Paint shadows.**
■ **Add colour to the
water.**

■ *Blow painting*

● HAVE READY
thin paint
straws, one for each child
non-absorbent paper
spoon
newspaper
● GET SET
Spread newspaper on flat
surface. Place paper on
top.
Using spoon, drip paint
onto paper.
● GO
Blowing gently through
straw, spread paint around
paper to make patterns.
Dry flat.

Other things to try
■ **When paint is dry
add details to picture
with felt tipped pens or
crayons.**

10

■ *Crayon resist*

● HAVE READY
crayons in light colours
paper
broad brushes
thin paint in a dark colour
newspaper
● GET SET
Make a pad with several sheets of newspaper. Place drawing paper on top.
● GO
Press down with crayons to make a thick, waxy drawing.
Cover drawing with paint.
Dry flat.

Other things to try
■ *Make a magic drawing by using a white candle to draw on white paper. A picture will magically appear when paint is applied.*

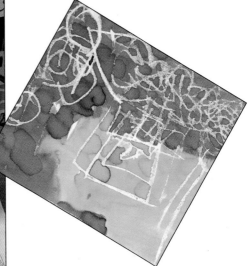

■ *Bubble painting*

● HAVE READY
powder´ paint or dye
dishwashing liquid
bowls or plastic containers
drinking straws
paper

● GET SET
Put some dishwashing liquid into a separate bowl for each colour.
Mix sufficient paint with a small quantity of water and add to dishwashing liquid to make a strong colour.
IT IS VERY IMPORTANT TO MAKE SURE THE CHILD KNOWS HOW TO BLOW THROUGH A STRAW BEFORE THIS NEXT STEP.

● GO
Put straw in liquid and keep blowing until bubbles rise higher than sides of bowl.
You can make a fabulous print of your bubbles by placing a sheet of paper gently on top of bubbles, without breaking them. Repeat this last step for each colour. Dry painting flat.

Other things to try
■ *Paint a picture around your bubble print with a paint brush and paint.*

■ *Foil painting*

● HAVE READY
foil
acrylic or tempera paint
liquid soap
brushes
● GET SET
Cut foil to painting size.
If using tempera, add 2-3
drops of liquid soap to
paint.
● GO

Other things to try
- ■ *Use cellophane instead of foil*
- ■ *Paint with thin brushes*

■ *Foil etching*

● HAVE READY   tempera paint in a dark colour
foil   liquid soap
cardboard   broad brush
tape   pencil or twig
● GET SET
Mix 2-3 drops of liquid soap with tempera paint. Secure foil to cardboard
with tape.
● GO
Brush paint to cover foil. Let dry. Using stick, scratch dry paint from foil to
make patterns or picture. Be careful not to break foil.

■ *Wet paper painting*

● HAVE READY
paper
water
sponge
thin paint
small spoons
brushes

● GET SET
On flat surface, wet paper thoroughly with water.

● GO
Drip paint onto wet paper with brush or spoon. Allow colours to blend.
Children may wish to go further, using a clean brush to mix colours
and develop patterns.
Dry flat.

Other things to try
■ *Using paste instead of water, spread paste with a broad brush.*

■ *Mixing colours*

● HAVE READY
powder paint in blue, red, yellow, black and white
spoons
metal patty pan tray or small plastic containers

water
brushes
sponge
paper

● GET SET
Have paper ready for painting and small quantities of powder paint.

● GO
Spoon very small amount of chosen colours of paint powder into a
container. Dip brush into water and mix powder to make paint. Use this
brush for painting. Wash brushes in clean water between mixes.

Other things to try
■ *Use liquid vegetable dyes or food colourings, adding colour with an eye dropper.*

■ *Blots and ...*

● HAVE READY
paint
brush, spoon or flat stick
paper
● GET SET
Fold paper in half then open it out
flat. Place paper on flat surface.
● GO
With brush, spoon or stick put
drops of paint on one half of paper,
beginning near fold. Fold paper
again and rub palms of hands over
paper, starting at fold and working
out to edges. Open paper out to
see the colourful blot.

Other things to try

■ *Cut out shapes to decorate a wall, hang in the breeze or fly on a mobile.*
■ *Make blots on small pieces of firm paper and use these for cards and gift tags.*

Butterflies

Make a wonderful rainbow butterfly in exactly the same way as the blots on page 15 by putting the paint along the fold of the paper for the body and arranging the colour where you want the wings to be. You can paint the feelers on later if you like. Cut out your butterflies and hang them up to fly in the breeze.

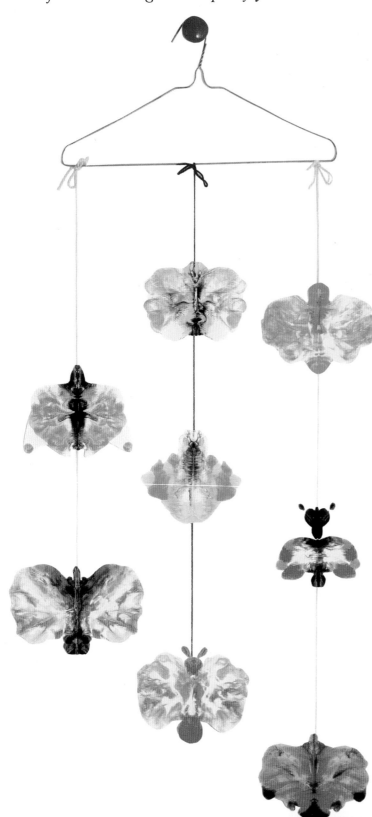

String painting

● HAVE READY
paint
string or wool
brushes
clip-type clothes pegs
paper

● GET SET
Cut lengths of string or wool 30-50 cm long.
Lay paper on a flat surface.

● GO
Holding one end of string with a peg, dip string into paint. You may need a brush to help coat string completely. Drape strings onto paper, making patterns. Lift strings off. Dry flat.

Other things to try
■ *Fold paper as for blot painting. Lay painted string on one side of paper, leaving peg hanging over edge. Fold paper again and holding firmly with one hand, pull string out from inside paper with other hand. Open paper and repeat process with same or different colours.*

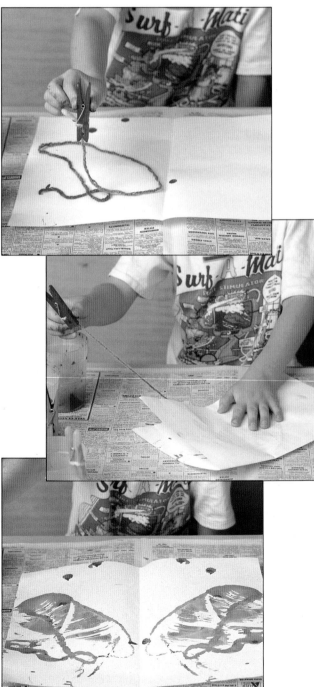

■ *People painting*

● HAVE READY
paper, large sheet or roll
crayon
paint
brushes
scissors (optional)
● GET SET
Place child-sized sheet of
paper on ground.
Draw around child,
making body outline.
● GO
Paint portrait inside
outline.
Figure can be cut out and
used in play or as a
wonderful decoration.

Other things to try
■ *Make a family of 'people' including baby, adults
and even a favourite teddy.*
■ *Decorate 'people' with scraps of materials,
coloured paper, wool and odds and ends of fabric for
clothes, hair, eyes and so on.*

Robbie

■ *Mural people*

● HAVE READY
same list of items as for *People painting*
tape or pegs

● GET SET
Make several 'people' on length of paper or tape individual pictures together to make a mural.

● GO
Cut holes for faces.
Suspend the mural, perhaps from a clothesline or between two trees, so that children can stand behind it with their faces peeping through.

Other things to try
■ *Use an old white bed sheet instead of paper.*
■ *Children can bring the mural to life, singing songs and telling stories as if acting out the story of the mural. An adult will often have to ask questions and get the singing started.*

Paper chains

● HAVE READY
a completed drawing or painting
ruler
pencil
scissors
paste or stapler
● GET SET
Turn drawing over and draw lines
dividing it into strips. Cut along lines.
Older children may manage this
alone but a younger child will need
help.
● GO
Make a loop by fixing ends with glue
or staples.
Add other strips, making interlocking
loops.

C hildren love the 'feel' of finger painting and of covering large areas with paint. Most of all they love the freedom to be messy without Mum getting cross!

Some children may be a little reluctant at first, so try these hints for starting a hesitant beginner. Wetting the child's hands with water before they start, using a light coloured paint mixed with liquid soap or using warm finger paint can all work to encourage that first step. For those who really don't like having dirty hands, rub on a hand cream before painting and put liquid soap or soap flakes in the paint. This makes removing the paint quickly a very simple matter.

Handprints

● HAVE READY
finger paint
flat dishes
paper
water and sponge
soapy water and towel
● GET SET
Put paint in flat dishes.
Moisten table surface, before placing paper on it, to stop paper slipping.
● GO
Put a hand in paint then place it firmly onto paper to make print. Make
hand prints in same or different colours, taking care to wash hands
between colour changes.

Other things to try
■ *Print hands onto*
fabric to make a wall
hanging.
■ *Set paint dishes on*
ground and make foot
prints.
■ *Cut out paper hands*
and feet and hang them
as mobiles.

What you need

Finger paint Finger paint can be bought commercially or you can make your own following our simple recipes opposite. Paints can be coloured with vegetable dyes, food colouring or powdered paint. Begin by making your own paste or starch or you can add colouring to wallpaper paste made at double strength. Take care not to use a paste that contains fungicide. Children love to play with mud and, believe it or not, mud makes a great medium for finger painting.

Paper If the finger painting is to be done on paper, choose large firm sheets (it does not have to be white). Remember, the paper must be strong enough to cope with the squeezing and squelching. Moistening the table top with water, before laying the paper on it, will hold the paper in place.

Covers and protectors Finger painting is messy so you will need to provide covering for the floor that is disposable or easily cleaned. The ideal covering for the floor is newspaper, which can be easily gathered up and disposed of. If you have the space, encourage your child to work outdoors — it does away with most clean-up problems. Painting aprons or old clothes, with sleeves which can be pushed up, are essential.

A low table Any flat surface will do and one is best that can be easily cleaned or covered with plastic or waterproof material.

A bucket of soapy water, sponge and towel Place these nearby for children to use before they move away and to clean the table before the paint dries.

Space Provide somewhere to hang or lay paintings flat to dry.

HINT
Liquid soap added to the paint will make hand cleaning easier.
Disinfectant added to the paint will ensure that it will keep for a few days or you can store it in the refrigerator.
A small quantity of cold water poured on top of finger paint will stop a skin forming.

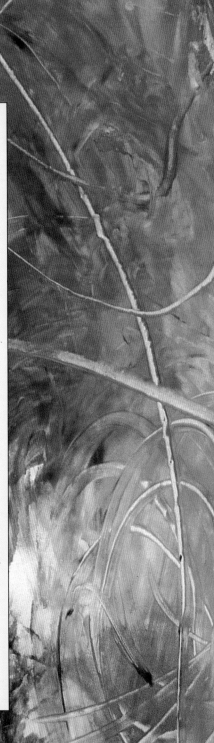

Cornflour paste
(makes a small quantity)
- ◼ 1 heaped tablespoon cornflour
- ◼ water
- ◼ colouring

Mix cornflour with a little cold water to make a smooth white paste.
Pour on boiling water, stirring rapidly, until mixture is thick, clear and smooth.
(If it doesn't thicken, cook it until it does.)
Add colour.

Cornflour paste
(makes a larger quantity)
- ◼ 1 part cornflour
- ◼ 3 parts water
- ◼ colouring

Mix cornflour in a little cold water to make a smooth white paste.
Add to water that is boiling, stirring constantly.
Return saucepan to heat and boil until mixture clears.
Add colour.

Starch
You may need to vary this recipe a little, depending on the brand of starch you use.
- ◼ 1 part dry starch
- ◼ 2 parts water
- ◼ colouring

Mix starch with a little water to make a paste.
Add boiling water, stirring constantly. (If it doesn't thicken, bring to boil on stove.)
Add colouring.

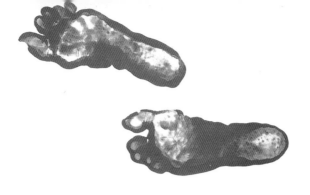

Footprints

● HAVE READY
large sheet of paper
tape
finger paint
flat dish or tray
bucket of soapy water and towel
chair
● GET SET
Tape paper to ground at both ends or secure it with blocks or some other suitable weights.
Place paint in dish at one end of paper.
● GO
Paint can be very slippery so it is important to hold child's hand as they stand in paint and then walk along paper to make prints.
Keep the bucket of soapy water nearby for washing feet.

Other things to try

▢ **Try making prints with washable soles of shoes.**
▢ **Make foot prints on paths, using water instead of paint.**

▢ **Foot painting can be done directly onto paper or a print can be made later. Work on a waterproof surface, such as a plastic sheet, and spoon paint directly onto it. Sit the child on a chair so they can use their feet to make pictures and patterns in the paint.**

Finger painting

● HAVE READY

finger paint
bowls or containers
spoons

strong paper
water and
sponge

● GET SET

Spoon paint into bowls or containers.
Sponge table lightly with water and place paper on top.
The damp surface will prevent paper from slipping.
Spoon paint from containers onto paper.

● GO

Blend colours to make patterns and pictures using all of
hands. Remove painting to dry. Wash hands and
painting surface.

Other things to try

*Instead of working directly onto paper, children
love to paint directly onto a table top. Then, with
clean, dry hands they can lay the sheet of paper
onto the painting, gently patting or rubbing over the
surface. The paper is then lifted carefully off the
paint and the printed pattern is revealed.*

*Try making patterns with spoon handles, forks,
iceblock sticks, cotton reels, sponges and
cardboard combs, cut to make a variety of effects.*

*To achieve changes
in texture add salt,
sawdust or rice to the
paint, to vary the 'feel'.
Or mix in some earth,
instead of colour, for
'mud painting'.*

A t first children enjoy the action of drawing without attaching any special significance to the marks and symbols. Later, they may name and identify the scribbles though you will not necessarily recognise them. Finally symbols and patterns are developed and repeated and the cat actually starts to look like one and Daddy has one head not two!

The best way for a child to start drawing is with the paper firmly secured on the floor or table. Later drawing can be done on a vertical surface, such as an easel, or on paper fixed to the wall.

Start with a sheet of paper, about 25cm x 20cm, then as skills and concentration develop provide larger sheets and introduce a variety of colours and textures in the paper.

Felt-tipped pens give a great choice of colours and flow very easily for young children. They can be used on most surfaces, including wax paper, plastic and fabric. However children must learn to replace the cap on each pen after use, as they dry out quickly. Water colour pens, not permanent colour, are most appropriate for this age, as the paint is washable.

Felt-tipped pens

● HAVE READY
variety of pens
paper
newspaper
● GET SET
Place newspaper or cardboard underneath paper as colours often bleed through.
● GO

Other things to try

■ Draw a tiny drawing on a balloon before blowing it up. Then blow up the balloon and watch the drawing grow!

■ Draw patterns around the edges of sheets of notepaper and around envelopes to match. Fold the notepaper in half to make a greeting card or stationery.

■ Draw a shape in one colour. Draw around it again and again and again, changing colours each time.

■ Lay bottles and jars of different sizes on their sides and draw around the outside, then fill in the outline with anything you fancy - jelly beans, ants, worms, monsters…!

Chalk drawing

● HAVE READY
light chalk and dark paper or
cardboard
OR dark chalk and light paper or
cardboard
soapy water
sponge
towel
● GET SET
Keep soapy water and sponge
handy so hands can be kept clean
during drawing.
● GO

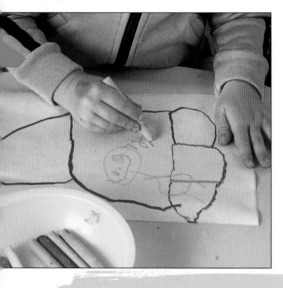

Other things to try

■ *Try drawing on wet paper for a*
very different effect.
■ *Mix one-third of a cup of sugar* *in a cup of hot water. When cool,*
wet chalk by dipping repeatedly
into sugar solution while
drawing.

Above left: Chalk drawing on wet paper
Above: Drawing with wet chalk

Crayon drawing

Non-toxic, kindergarten-type
crayons, about 150 mm in diameter,
are easiest for the youngest children
to hold and control. Thinner crayons
can be added later, but they break
more easily and are more tiring to
use.

● HAVE READY
a variety of coloured, non-toxic
crayons
suitable paper
● GET SET
Secure paper to table surface.
● GO

Crayon rubbing

● HAVE READY
crayons
leaves
thin paper
cardboard

● GET SET
Remove paper from crayons.
Arrange leaves on cardboard or a flat surface.
Tape paper in place over leaves.

● GO
Rub side of crayon lightly all over paper. Lift paper off to reveal shape and texture of leaves.

Other things to try

■ *Place familiar objects, such as keys, coins and combs, under the paper.*
■ *Try using embossed wallpapers, paper doilies and corrugated cardboard or wriggly things, such as rubber bands, string and shoe laces.*
■ *Take paper outside and rub it on concrete paths, brick walls, bark and any other interesting surface.*

Jigsaws

You may need to help with the cutting out on this one. Two simple pieces may be enough for the youngest child. Increase the number of pieces and complexity of shapes for the older child.

● HAVE READY

a completed drawing   cardboard
paste or glue   crayon
broad brush   scissors

● GET SET
Cover back of drawing with paste.
Glue drawing onto cardboard, smoothing out all wrinkles.

● GO

*P*aper is the most exciting and inexpensive craft material. It can be folded, glued, painted on, drawn on, cut up and sewn with great ease. Children of all ages enjoy working with paper, scissors and glue to bring their imagination to life and, best of all, paper need not cost anything at all! Have a 'treasure' box or drawer, filled with paper of all kinds. Ask friends and family to save special papers for you, such as gift wrapping or wallpaper.

Provide your child with a pair of scissors, suitable to their age and size. Cutting isn't easy. Children need to understand about opening and closing the scissors and how to hold and move the paper. Make sure the paper is not too thin (it will be hard to hold and scissors will slip), or too thick (small children will simply not be strong enough to manage). Give them lots of practice, cutting up magazines or newspapers. Later all the pieces can be stuck on cardboard or paper to make a picture!

What you need

Paper All kinds of paper are wonderful for craft work. Collect a variety including different colours and textures such as: absorbent, water repellant; tissue; gift wrapping; wallpaper; shopping bags; magazines; butchers' paper; crepe paper; newspaper; paper plates; doilies; greeting cards; foil; cellophane.

Scissors Children start by tearing paper but soon move on to cutting. It is important that children's scissors **will** actually cut. Give them small scissors, about 10 cm long, with rounded tips and remember there are both right- and left-handed scissors available.

Paste There are many very suitable pastes and glues on the market. They should be non-toxic and easy to handle without too much mess. Of course, it is quite simple to make your own paste and we have included two recipes on page 41 for you to try.

Choose the right strength of paste or glue to suit the paper. It is very disappointing for a child to have a special creation fall apart. For light paper items, commercial pastes and wallpaper pastes (without fungicide) or one of our homemade pastes are suitable. For heavier items use P.V.A. (polyvinyl adhesive), clear hobby or craft glues.

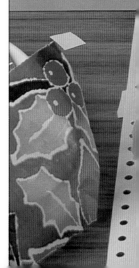

Paper collage

Coloured papers, such as old paintings, magazines, foil and greeting cards can provide a great variety of colours and textures. Children can tear or cut their own pieces of paper or you can pre-cut various shapes, sizes and colours.

● HAVE READY
firm paper or cardboard	scissors
paste	variety of papers
brush	containers
	damp cloth or sponge

● GET SET
Sort paper into colours, shapes, types and size and place in containers.
Place a large piece of paper or cardboard on table as collage base.
Choose pieces of paper and tear or cut as necessary.
● GO
Brush paste onto back of paper pieces.
Stick in position on base to make patterns or a picture.

Other things to try
■ **Draw or paint over the collage or on the base before beginning the collage.**

Mosaics

Mosaics take time and patience so begin with a small one.

● HAVE READY
scraps of coloured paper of any size
firm paper or cardboard
scissors
paste
brush
● GET SET
Tear paper into tiny pieces.
● GO
Apply paste to a small area of firm paper or cardboard backing and stick down scraps of paper to form pattern or picture.

Other things to try
■ **Draw on backing sheet first then paste pieces of paper in place over drawing.**

■ *Picture fun*

● HAVE READY
old magazines
firm paper or cardboard
crayons or felt-tipped pens
scissors
paste
brush
● GET SET
Cut out parts of different
people from magazines.
● GO
Rearrange the parts and
paste them onto
background to make new
people.
Draw in extra details if you
wish.

Other things to try
■ *Put together new animals and give your pet a name.*
■ *Youngest children can begin by exchanging heads on two bodies, then change legs as well. Later on you can increase the number of people and make up stories about them.*

■ *Snowflakes*

For very young children it is best to begin with thick paper, folded in half only. Increase number of folds with increasing age and skill level. Young children may prefer to tear the design rather than cut it.

● HAVE READY
squares of paper
scissors
● GET SET
Fold paper square in half and then half again. Fold diagonally to form triangle.
● GO
Cut out design all around edges.
Unfold paper to reveal snowflake.

Other things to try
■ *Older children can make more folds before cutting.*
■ *Different shaped papers can be used to make doilies.*
■ *Drawings and paintings can be used to make placemats and colourful decorations.*

Fold, dip and dye

● HAVE READY
paper towelling or napkins
food colouring or vegetable dye
containers — one for each colour

● GET SET
Mix colouring or vegetable dye with water in shallow containers.

● GO
Fold paper in half and then half again.
Dip each corner of paper into a colour, one at a time.
Unfold paper to reveal design. Allow to dry flat.

Other things to try
■ *Make more folds before dipping.*
■ *Dip folded snowflakes into more colours.*

Paper weaving

A paper weaving can be as 'pretty as a picture'. Weaving doesn't have to be completed in one go, but can be put aside for later. Start with paper that is not easily broken, such as crepe paper and cellophane.

● HAVE READY
strips of paper
frame (see instructions below)
string or wool
● GET SET
To prepare the frame, hammer nails, equally spaced, across top and bottom of an old picture frame. The side of a cardboard carton will also work as a frame, with Vs cut into edges at top and bottom. Make a small frame at first until children are comfortable with the weaving.
● GO
Secure string or wool at top left corner and wind it around nails, or through the Vs, from top to bottom, making parallel threads. Secure at end. Weave paper in and out, across threads.

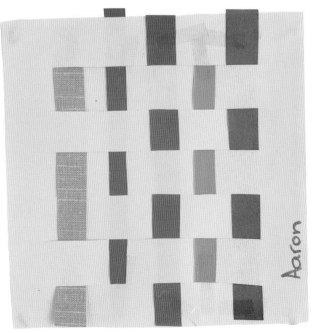

All-paper weaving

This activity is best kept for the child who already knows how to weave.

● HAVE READY
sturdy paper
strips of paper
scissors
paste, tape, glue or staples
● GET SET
Fold sheet of sturdy paper in half. Starting from fold, cut slits across paper, stopping about 2 cm from edge. (Slits need not be straight or even.)
● GO
Weave paper strips in and out of slits.
Glue, tape or staple each strip at both ends, before starting with next strip. This holds weaving in place.

A collage is an arrangement of materials that are glued onto a flat surface, such as a piece of paper or cardboard. The wider the variety of objects and materials that are used, the more interesting the finished work will be. There is no limit to what you can use, so set aside a box to store interesting bits and pieces of fabric, string, paper, twigs and leaves. Choosing the raw materials for a collage is half the fun.

You can select a particular colour theme or type of material to be used. It is also interesting to work on a coloured or oddly-shaped background. Decide whether the background is itself part of the collage or whether it is to be totally covered.

Try making a collage with a particular theme, such as 'summer', 'animals', 'blue' or 'cars'.

Some collages make wonderful wall decorations while others, such as the city scene in our chapter on Junk, can be a marvellous play area, to be enjoyed in conjunction with other toys.

You will need

Materials Keep a large variety of materials available to make the collage but don't provide too many types of things at one time. Use this list of suggested materials as a starting point, but remember the list is really endless: bark; beads; bottle tops and caps; small boxes; buttons; cardboard; confetti; cotton wool; ferns; flowers; foil; grass; lace; leather; leaves; lids; pebbles; ribbon; rope; sand; sawdust; seeds; shells; stamps; dead matches; dried beans; dried flowers; crushed egg shells; fabric; feathers; net; nuts; pasta; paper; patty pans; streamers; straw; string; toothpicks; twigs; woodshavings; wool.

Staples and tape Masking tape is easiest for young children to manage. If possible put tape on a dispenser.

Crayons, felt-tipped pens, pencils or paint

Scissors Provide a good pair of small scissors that cut easily.

Containers Put collage materials into various containers, so that it is easy to pick and choose from them. Any clean container will do.

Paste Pastes and glues need to be strong enough to hold the materials in place. For light pieces use homemade pastes, commercial or wallpaper paste and for heavier ones try P.V.A. (polyvinyl adhesive), clear wood, hobby or craft glues. Glues can be applied in small squeeze bottles or by brush. You can also make your own paste using the simple recipes opposite.

Belinda

CORNFLOUR PASTE
- 1/2 cup cornflour
- 1/2 cup cold water
- boiling water

Mix cold water and cornflour to make smooth white paste.
Quickly add boiling water while stirring. Stir until paste is clear.
Add disinfectant, if paste is to be kept, and refrigerate.

PLAIN FLOUR PASTE
- 1/2 cup plain flour
- 3/4 cup cold water

Mix water and flour to make a smooth paste. Boil over low heat for several
minutes, stirring continuously.
Thin with cold water, if necessary. Add disinfectant, if paste is to be kept,
and refrigerate.

■ *Collage ideas*

Collage requires the gathering of lots and lots of interesting objects and materials of different textures. If you have a particular colour or theme in mind, keep an eye out wherever you go for collage 'treasures'. A visit to the beach or the park can provide a wealth of raw materials, as can searching through the drawers and cupboards at home.

Theme collages are often the most fun. Collecting can become a wonderful activity all on its own and will test the ingenuity of the whole family. Base a collage on the seaside, a farm, an airport or even a trip to the moon!

W onderful puppets can certainly enrich a child's play. Often, however, there may be as much pleasure in the making of the puppet or a puppet theatre, as in the playing. Children can create a new friend, a monster, a cat, a figment of their imagination or simply have hours of fun. Remember an 'end product' isn't always necessary.

A child's puppet can be fantastic or ordinary, it can laugh or cry, jump or sleep, disappear and reappear. Most importantly, puppets are a wonderful vehicle for the expression of ideas and imagination. A shy, four year old can present a wonderful play, where all the talking is done by someone else!

A puppet can be as simple as a face drawn on a finger and given a name and personality. An older child, with more skill and suitable materials can make quite a complex creation.

The puppets on the following pages are intended only as sparks for the imagination. Don't reproduce them exactly. Much of the joy of puppet-making and play is in making something that is quite unique.

What you need

Scrap materials old socks and gloves; tubes and boxes; sticks; pine cones; paper bags; paper plates; balloons; wool; cotton wool; paper and cardboard are just a few things to save for making puppets.

Paste, glue, tape or staples

Scissors Provide a good pair of small scissors that cut easily.

Crayons, felt-tipped pens and paint

Space Provide an area that can be cleaned easily and a cloth or sponge for sticky fingers.

Finger puppets

● **HAVE READY**
paper, felt or material
bits and pieces of cotton wool; ribbons; material; lace
glue
scissors
felt-tipped pens

● GET SET
Make a finger stall by cutting a shape out of paper, felt
or fabric about 9 cm x 6 cm. Roll up and glue down (or
sew down) edge, leaving bottom end open for finger.
Glue or paint on a face and add clothes and hair.
● GO

■ *Walking puppets*

● HAVE READY
cardboard
felt-tipped pens
scissors
glue or paste
bits and pieces such as fabric, wool,
cotton wool and so on

● GET SET
Draw a figure or paste a completed
drawing onto cardboard.
Cut around figure and then cut out
holes for 'legs', large enough for a
finger to poke through.
Decorate puppet by adding facial
features, hair and clothes.

● GO
Put fingers through the holes and
walk puppet along.

■ *Paper plate puppet*

● HAVE READY
paper plates
felt-tipped pens
collage bits and pieces
glue or strong paste
scissors
tape
sticks

● GET SET
Decorate a plate with pens and
glued-on bits and pieces to make
puppet's head. Tape a stick to back
of plate for a handle.

● GO

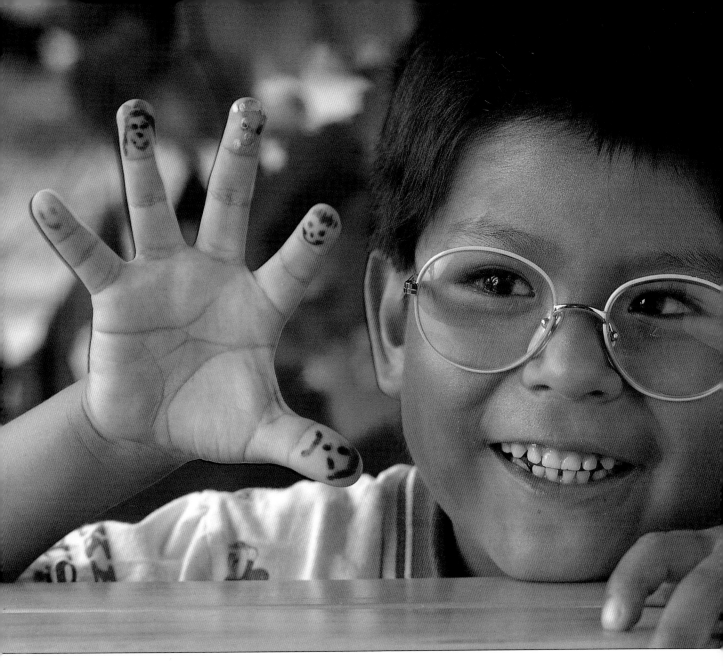

■ *Finger family*

● HAVE READY
felt-tipped pens (not permanent colour!)
● GET SET
Draw friendly and ferocious faces on palm side of fingers, so puppet fingers can bow and nod.
● GO
Find a shelf, bannister or upturned box and on with the show!

■ *Paper bag puppet*

● HAVE READY
paper bags
felt-tipped pens or crayons
bits and pieces of fabric, wool and so on

glue or strong paste, stapler
scissors
stick or cardboard cylinder
tape or elastic band

● GET SET
Draw a face on paper bag.
Fill bag with scrunched up paper.
Attach bag to stick or cardboard cylinder with elastic band or tape.
● GO

Other things to try

■ *A small empty bag can go over child's hand without a handle.*
■ *Make puppet out of an old sock, decorated with a face and hair.*

Puppet on a stick

● HAVE READY

drawing or painting   tape
scissors   stick

● GET SET

Cut out puppet figure or head from the painting. You
may need to paste it onto cardboard if paper is too light.
Tape stick behind figure.

● GO

Other things to try

■ *Use a piece of decorated
cardboard instead of a stick.*
■ *Make clothes out of paper or
material for puppet and secure
with glue, tape or a pipe-cleaner.*

Finger people

● HAVE READY
felt-tipped pens
material and paper scraps
scissors
elastic bands
● GET SET
Draw a face on one finger.
Wrap paper or material around finger for clothes and secure with rubber band.
Tear or cut out a circle of paper for a hat. Tear a small cross in centre of circle. Push finger into tear to make hat.
● GO

Rubber glove puppet

● HAVE READY
rubber glove
felt-tipped pens
● GET SET
Cut finger tips off rubber glove and draw faces on them with coloured pens.
Glue wool on puppets for hair.
● GO

KITCHEN PUPPETS

Familiar kitchen items can become terrific puppets in the wink of an eye. Try some of these great ideas to start you off.

■ Stella Strainer

● HAVE READY
strainer
paper
crayons or felt-tipped pens
scissors
glue or liquid starch
wool
● GET SET
Make eyes, mouth and nose out of paper and stick onto strainer.
Thread wool through metal holes to make hair.
● GO
Perhaps Stella could sing a song or two?

■ Terrible Tongs

● HAVE READY
felt-tipped pens or
crayons
tape
kitchen tongs
egg carton
● GET SET
Tear or cut cups from egg carton.
Draw eyes on as shown.
Tape eyes into place on tongs.
● GO
Animate the 'terrible snapping tong monster' and don't forget the sound effects.

Sam Spoon

● HAVE READY
wooden spoon or serving spoon
paper towelling or cloth
tape, elastic band or ribbon
● GET SET
Arrange towelling or cloth around
handle for clothes.
Secure with tape, band or ribbon.
● GO

Other things to try
■ *If it is an old spoon
and no longer needed in
the kitchen, you could
paint a face on it with
felt-tipped pens.*

Dishy Dolly

● HAVE READY
dishmop
paper
scissors
paste or glue
cloth
elastic band
felt-tipped pens (not permanent
colour!)
● GET SET
Tear or cut out paper eyes and
mouth and stick them onto mop.
Place cloth around mop and
gather at 'neck'.
Hold dress in place with elastic
band.
● GO

Other things to try
■ *Cover mop with cloth or
handkerchief and secure with
elastic band. Draw puppet face
on cloth.*

THEATRES & SHOWS

You've made your puppet and now it's on with the show! And a show needs a stage of some kind. Your home is probably full of potential 'theatres', such as a table, turned on its side, a window sill or the stair railing. With only a little more effort you can make many simple stages for a puppet show. Cut the centre out of an old sheet and hang it up on the washing line or cut the bottom out of a cardboard carton and you have a TV set. For the very simplest puppet show, make a hole in the bottom of a paper cup and pop up your cast of characters.

Children like an audience for their puppets — someone to clap and cheer, ask questions or sing along. A 'show' can last from ten seconds to ten minutes as children experiment and find out what 'theatre' is all about.

Giant puppet

● HAVE READY
firm paper
stapler
crayons, paint or felt-tipped pens
newspaper
cardboard cylinder
tape
old clothes
● GET SET
Cut two sheets of paper the same size to make the head.
Staple them together, leaving a hole at neck. Paint or draw in face. Fill head with scrunched-up newspaper.
Tape head to a long cardboard cylinder.
● GO

Other things to try
■ *Dress the puppet like a scarecrow with another cardboard cylinder through the arms of a shirt and taped to the other cylinder at shoulder level.*
■ *Add streamers for hair.*

JUNK

*U*nwanted bits and pieces, that so often get thrown away, are a great source of raw material for making things. Check our list of creative junk and remember — if it's safe and you have room, store it don't trash it! Storing materials for potential treasures can be a problem but it's one worth solving.

You will need

strong glue or tape for joining heavy items.

scissors

paint, crayons and felt-tipped pens for decorating

bits and pieces for trimming, such as wool, feathers and so on

Junk list — some ideas to start you saving				
balls	keys	fasteners	paper	cardboard cylinders
balloons	cards	sticks and twigs	paper plates	string
bark	burnt matches	lace	pine cones	stockings
bottle caps and tops	cellophane	leather	pipe cleaners	tinsel
bottles - plastic	clothes hangers	lids	pegs	net
boxes - all sizes	corks	washers	ribbons	wheels
buttons	cotton wool	jewellery	rope	wood offcuts
cans	plastic containers	paper bags	shells	wool
cardboard cartons	drinking straws	paper clips	spools	yoghurt cartons

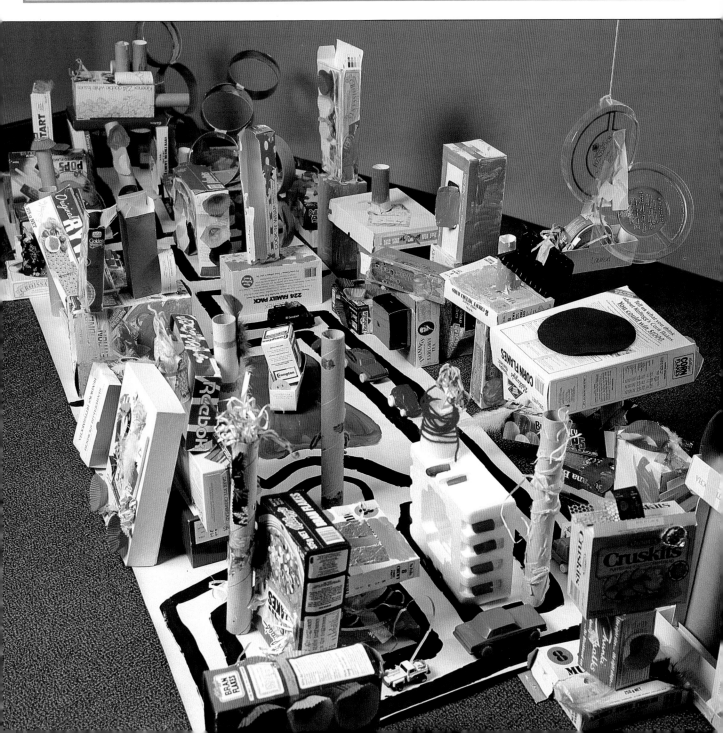

JUNK BAND

Making music is fun. Making your own instruments to make music with is even more so.

◼ *Strings to pluck*

● HAVE READY
cardboard boxes, such as tissue or shoe boxes
big elastic bands in various widths
● GET SET
Cut a hole in the lid of a shoe box.
Stretch elastic bands around box, over the hole.
Pluck bands, making a 'tune' with different sized bands.
● GO

Other things to try
◼ **To make a guitar, cut a hole in one end of a firm box. Fit a cardboard cylinder through the hole and tape it into place. Place elastic bands lengthways around box. A stick squeezed under the bands at each end of the box will improve the sound.**

◼ *Bells*

● HAVE READY
foil bottle tops
wool or string
blunt-tipped or darning needle
● GET SET
* Thread needle and tie knot in end of wool.
Make holes in bottle tops and thread onto wool. Younger children will need holes made for them.
*Remove needle and tie ends of wool together.
● GO

◼ *Bottlephone*

● HAVE READY
glass bottles   vegetable colouring and eye dropper
water and jug   metal spoon or stick
● GET SET
Using a jug, fill each bottle to a different level with water.
Put a drop of colouring in each bottle.
Place bottles in a row.
● GO
Strike bottles gently to hear different sounds. See how different levels of water affect the note. Play a tune and sing along.

Heavy metal music

● HAVE READY
clothesline
metal spoon or stick
string
metal objects such as kitchen utensils; metal tubing;
bolts; large screws and so on
● GET SET
Tie metal objects onto clothesline so they hang freely.
● GO
See how different objects make very different sounds.

Other things to try
■ *Put on a tape of a favourite song in the background to play along with.*

Drums

● HAVE READY
boxes, tins or plastic containers
sticks, pieces of dowelling or wooden spoons
scissors or a hole punch
string or ribbon
● GET SET
Make two holes, opposite one another, near the top of your drum.
Cut string or ribbon, long enough to go around the neck and thread through the holes.
Make knots in both ends of string, inside drum, so strap doesn't pull out.
● GO

Other things to try

■ *Make other drums which can be played while seated or carried on one arm and played with a stick or hand.*
■ *Make a whole drum kit for a rock band drummer.*

Maracas

● HAVE READY
paper plates
dried beans, pasta or rice for rattle
stapler
stick
tape
● GET SET
Cover a paper plate with an upturned plate of same size.
Staple around the edge, about three quarters of the way around.
Put beans inside plates and complete stapling around edge.
You can tape a stick to the plates, or between the plates to be a handle.
● GO

Shakers

● HAVE READY
plastic bottles, small tins or plastic containers
things to rattle such as rice; sand; pebbles; seeds or pasta
strong glue
tape
● GET SET
Put a small quantity of rattly objects into an empty bottle or container. Glue or tape lid into place. This is important for very young children for whom loose small items can be dangerous. Paint or decorate the outside of the shaker.
● GO
Shake up the rhythm section of your very own band.

Other things to try
■ *Leave clear plastic shakers undecorated so contents can be 'seen as well as heard'.*
■ *Let children experiment making sounds using different amounts of filling in similar containers, same filling in different containers or different fillings.*

Tooters

● HAVE READY
cardboard cylinder
paper (greaseproof is quite good)
glue or paste and brush
elastic band
● GET SET
Put paste around outside of one end of cylinder.
Cover end with a piece of paper.
Hold paper in place with elastic band. Make a hole in paper.
● GO

Other things to try
■ *Use a very long cylinder for a different sound, such as that from an Aboriginal didgeridoo or a Swiss flugelhorn.*

P rinting is a little like magic! The shape of a familiar object is transferred onto another surface but in reverse. When printing, paint can be applied directly to the object with a brush, rolled over it with a roller or the object can be coated with paint on a pad.

The simplest kind of printing to begin with is with a pad. Before the child begins, demonstrate the steps for printing — a gentle dab on the paint pad, a look underneath to see if the shape is coated with paint and then a firm press onto the paper to make the print. Show that it is important not to move the shape sideways when pressing, in order to make a nice, clear print.

Start with items that are easily held by small hands, such as pieces of wood, cotton reels, plastic toys, bottle tops and cooking utensils. Pieces of sponge and fabric can be held with a clothespeg.

At first let children experiment with the action and make simple prints. Later as confidence grows they will be able to produce designs and pictures.

What you need

Shallow dish or tray Place a thin sponge or folded paper towel into the dish. Place the paint *under* the sponge or *on* the towelling and allow a few minutes for it to soak in.

Paints Those made with vegetable dyes or powdered paints are usually most successful.

Paper or cardboard Material to be printed, needs to be absorbent. Place a pad of folded newspaper underneath to protect the table.

Sponge or cloth

■ *Fruit and vegetable printing*

● HAVE READY
a variety of the following - potato; carrot; onion;
cauliflower; pepper; orange; lemon; apple
paint pad, tray and paint
paper
paper towel
knife

● GET SET
*Cut firm fruit or vegetables to create flat surfaces.
Place cut side down on paper towel.
Press flat side of object down onto paint pad, checking
that it is well-covered with paint.

● GO
Press object firmly onto paper to make print.

Other things to try
■ **Cut potato into geometrical shapes.**
■ **Older children can cut with a knife, or use a spoon, to make their own designs.**

■ *Spattering*

● HAVE READY
strainer or wire screen on a frame
tooth or nail brush
shallow dish
thin paint or dye
paper
objects for printing, such as leaves; grasses; paper doily;
paper shapes; kitchen utensils; and so on

● GET SET
Place objects on paper.
Dip brush in paint and tap off any excess.
Place strainer over objects.

● GO
Rub brush over wire, spattering paint over the object and
paper.
Allow painting to dry flat. Remove objects to reveal the
printed shapes beneath.

Leaf and object printing

● HAVE READY

leaves or textured objects, such as corrugated
cardboard, mesh, vegetable bags, lace, wool, string
cardboard
paste or glue
scissors
tray
thick paint and spoon
printing roller or paint roller
paper

● GET SET

Cut objects to size and arrange on cardboard. Glue in
place and allow to dry.
Spoon paint into tray and work roller in it until it is
covered with paint.
Roll paint onto objects so they are covered with paint.

● GO

Lay paper on top and pat or rub over the surface.
Carefully remove paper to reveal print on the underside.
Print can be repeated and more paint added in different
colours perhaps.

Other things to try
■ *Glue string around roller to add an unusual texture. Allow the glue to dry before making print.*
■ *Glue pieces of cardboard onto roller to make unusual patterns in the print.*

■ *Roller printing*

● HAVE READY
paint, pad and tray
paper
empty drink can, cardboard
cylinder, rolling pin, plastic bottle,
hair roller, jar lid, cotton reel, string
or wool and so on
cardboard
scissors
P.V.A. glue
● GET SET
Roll different items on paint pad.
● GO
Roll on paper to make patterns.

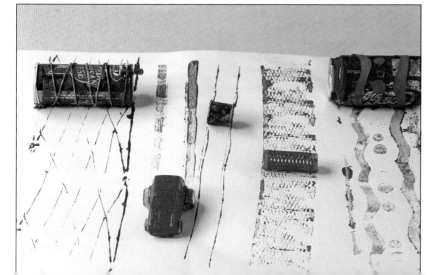

MODELLING

*H*olding, feeling, squeezing, pounding, pulling, pushing, pinching and patting — are the greatest fun! With dough and clay, children have the opportunity to do all these things and at the same time develop important muscles in their fingers and hands.

Modelling encourages the use of imagination, as children mould a fantasy world populated by their own creations. Dough can be re-used, changed around or re-worked completely. Objects can be quite temporary, or in the case of clay, be kept for a very long time.

Combine dough and clay models with other toys to create a whole world of fantasy or just make a pile of marbles for a playtime game.

Like a lot of children's activities, the end product of modelling is not as important as the joy of doing it. The role of the adult should be to provide the dough and the space to work in. Allow your children to experiment and play the game of creation.

You will need

Dough Dough can be plain or coloured. Children should experience both, and some will prefer one and some the other. Children love to mix colours together, watching a rainbow dough develop. There are a variety of recipes for making dough. The simplest, uncooked type children can make themselves, with a little help or supervision.

Covered table Moulding with dough can get quite messy, so provide a surface that can be easily cleaned and some old clothes to wear.

Flour in a shaker Dough gets sticky to handle so a little flour, to sprinkle over it while working, is a good idea.

■ *Cooked dough*

- ■ 2 cups plain flour
- ■ 1 cup salt
- ■ 2 tablespoons oil
- ■ 4 tablespoons cream of tartar
- ■ 2 cups water
- ■ colouring (optional)

In a saucepan, mix dry ingredients. Gradually add oil and water, stirring them in together. Cook on top of the stove for 2-5 minutes, stirring constantly. The dough is cooked when mixture leaves side of pan and forms a mass. Cooked dough will keep in a sealed container, in the refrigerator, for up to three months.

Other things to try

■ *Add some simple equipment to use with dough, such as rolling pin; biscuit cutters; blunt knitting needles; garlic press; plate for cutting around and so on.*

■ *Add texture to the dough by mixing in some rice, pasta or beans.*

■ *Add items to press into the dough to make patterns, such as a fork; cotton reel; lids; lace; leaves and sticks.*

■ *Uncooked dough*

- ■ 2 cups plain flour
- ■ 1 cup cooking salt
- ■ colouring (optional)
- ■ 2 tablespoons cooking oil
- ■ approximately 1 cup water
- ■ bowl
- ■ mixing spoon

Mix dry ingredients in bowl with spoon, add oil.
Add colouring to water in a jug. Add water to bowl, a little at a time, stirring at first, then mixing with hands and kneading.
Dough can be kept in a floured container or plastic bag. If you are planning to keep it for a week or more, put it in the refrigerator in an airtight container.

■ *Clay bake decorations*

Children can make this simple baker's clay with a little help and supervision. The quantities in the recipe must be used exactly as given. They cannot be halved or doubled.

● HAVE READY
4 cups plain flour, unsifted
1 cup salt
1 1/2 cups water
bowl
kitchen utensils, such as a rolling pin; blunt knife; fork; toothpicks; hair pins; wire or paper clips
paint and brushes
clear gloss enamel

● GET SET
Mix salt and flour in bowl.
Add water, mixing with fingers. If clay is too stiff, add a little more water. When mixed, take clay out of bowl and knead for about 4-5 minutes.

● GO
Roll and shape decorations and place on baking trays.
Insert hair pins, wire or paper clips into back of shape, to make hooks.
Bake in moderate oven at least one hour.
Decorations can be coloured with paint or pens and made more durable by painting with clear gloss enamel.

This is an alternative baker's clay that doesn't actually need baking.

● HAVE READY
2 cups bicarbonated soda
1 cup cornflour
1 1/2 cups cold water

● GET SET
Mix flour and soda.
Add water, mixing until smooth.
*Boil one minute, stirring frequently, until the texture is like mashed potato.
*Put on plate and cover with damp cloth until cool.
Knead and roll dough.

● GO
Shape decorations and allow to dry out before decorating.

■ *Clay*

You might be lucky enough to live in an area where you can find clay naturally in the earth. If you are not so fortunate you can buy modelling clay from pottery or craft shops. Work the clay with your fingers, like kneading, and slap and bang ('wedge') it on the table top to remove air bubbles. Keep working the clay in this way until the clay is soft. Roll the clay into balls and push a thumb into each ball. Fill the hole with water and cover with a damp cloth. This will keep your clay soft. If it does dry out, break it up and soak it in water for a day or two. When the clay is again soft, pour off the water and spread the clay out to dry a little. Clay will keep virtually indefinitely, especially if kept in an airtight container.

Clay is messy, so work on a surface that can be wiped clean. Have a spatula or scraper and a bowl of water nearby for cleaning up and washing hands.

Children can use the same equipment for clay as for dough. Leave clay somewhere out of the way to dry out, but not in the sun. Paint it later if you wish or varnish it with clear enamel.

C hildren love to gather and organise. Threading objects onto a cord or string is a great favourite. At first, provide objects for threading that are short with large holes and use a fairly stiff cord to thread them on. Plastic tubing, insulated electrician's wire, a shoelace with a stiff end or string with a wrapping of sticky-tape on the end are all excellent.

A bodkin or darning needle can also be useful, but make sure, after threading, that you tie the thread behind the eye so it can't come out.

When preparing material for threading, pre-cut the string and knot the end or tie the first object on so everything doesn't slip off the end.

■ *Paper beads*

● HAVE READY
old magazines
darning needle
wool or string
scissors
glue

● GET SET
Cut colour pages of magazines lengthways to make long triangles, about 5 cm wide at the base and 30 cm tall.
Cut cord for necklace and secure to needle.

● GO
Starting from the wide end of triangle, roll paper around the needle.
Put glue on the pointed end of the paper triangle and press down to complete bead.
Continue making beads on the needle and pushing them along the thread. When there are sufficient beads on the cord, tie the ends together securely.

Y ou will need some kind of frame or loom for weaving but it need not be an expensive one. A forked stick, cardboard box, polystyrene tray, chicken wire or paper plate are but a few ideas to try. Make sure the weaving and frame are not too large for the child to manage and that they are positioned to be easy to work on. Cover any sharp ends of the frame with tape.

Cut wool, string, paper and material in lengths, ready for weaving. And if using a bodkin or darning needle, tie the threads behind the eye, so they don't pull out.

■ *Weaving in a tree*

This type of weaving does not need to be formal. If you don't have a suitable tree to use, hang a branch inside for a very similar effect.

● HAVE READY
strips of material, wool or string
long grasses and reeds
feathers
strips of coloured paper
● GET SET
Find a suitable branch for the top and a smaller one for the bottom. Tie lengths of material, wool and string between the upper and lower branches.
● GO
Weave across these 'strings' using some of the materials we suggest and any others you can find around the house or garden.

Other things to try
■ *Once the basic weaving is complete, add dried flowers and leaves, twigs and interesting seed pods.*

 # *Ojo*

● HAVE READY
two long sticks or twigs
wool or string
● GET SET
Cut lengths of wool.
Cross two sticks and tie together
securely where they cross.
● GO
Weave wool under and over sticks,
working from centre to outside. Tie
ends of wool together to change
colours.

Other things to try
■ *Older children can weave the wool over one stick, then around and under the stick, then move wool to next stick, continuing from centre to outside, and tying wools to the sticks when changing colours. They may also be able to manage the wool in small balls instead of cut lengths.*

Weaving on a tray

● HAVE READY
polystyrene tray
knife
scissors
darning needle
wool; ribbon; strips of paper;
feathers and so on

● GET SET
*With a knife, cut a window in the
tray.
*Thread needle and tie knot.
Push needle through tray. Turn tray
over and pull thread through. On
opposite side of window, make a
similar hole and pull thread through.
Continue making parallel 'strings'
across the window. When finished
tie knot in wool and cut off any
excess.

● GO
Lengths of wool, paper or ribbon
can be woven across the frame to
complete the weaving. There is no
need for regular 'under-over'
weaving, an irregular texture is very
attractive.

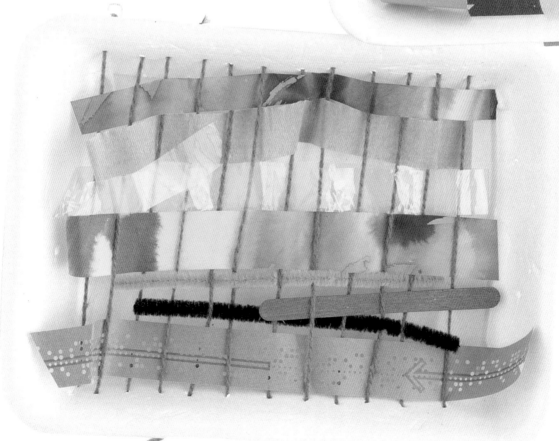

SEWING

*S*ewing is just another way of 'painting' a picture or making a design, using threads instead of paints. For very young children, sewing for the first time, it is best to begin with some firm open-weave fabric, such as hessian, or even a piece of polystyrene. You can draw the design onto the fabric first, if you prefer, or just 'draw' the picture with needle and thread.

● HAVE READY
wool
bodkin or darning needle
scissors
● GET SET
Cut length of wool.
*Thread needle and tie wool behind eye. Knot end of wool.
● GO
Sew freely over tray or fabric, pushing needle through and pulling up thread each time, before making next stitch.

Other things to try
■ *Draw a picture on fabric and follow line with stitches.*
■ *With a hole puncher, make holes in cardboard and sew around holes.*
■ *Draw on cardboard. Cut out drawing and make holes around the edge. Sew around your own 'sewing card'.*

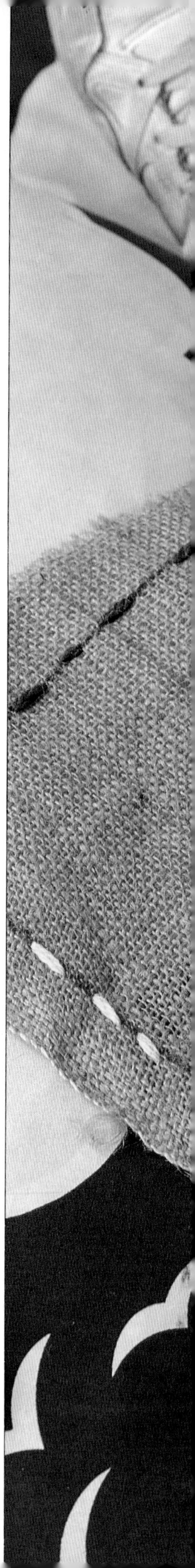

The Useful Box

This is a list of just some of the things you might like to collect and store for craft materials.

Paper of various kinds — newspaper; gift wrapping; wallpaper; cardboard; plain paper in different colours and foil.

Fabric — collect scraps of materials in as many different textures, colours and weights as you can.

Cardboard tubes, cylinders and boxes

Wool — try to have as many different types of wool as you can.

Old kitchen utensils — particularly strainers and wooden spoons, which make wonderful puppets, drumsticks and musical instruments.

Bottle tops

Ribbons, cords and string

Discarded costume jewellery

Shells

Bark, pine cones and interesting seeds

Buttons

Timber offcuts — make certain these are quite smooth and not likely to produce splinters.